W9-AVP-154

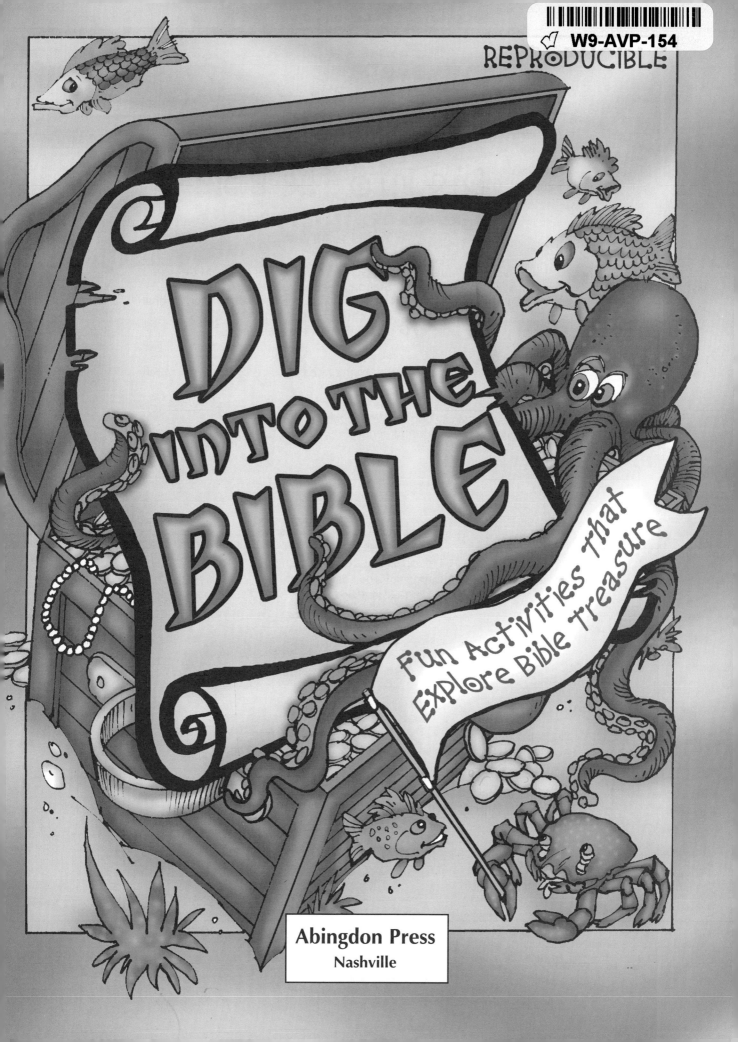

DIG INTO THE BIBLE

Fun Activities that Explore Bible Treasure

Abingdon Press

Nashville

Dig Into the Bible

Unless otherwise noted, Scripture quotations are from the
New Revised Standard Version of the Bible,
copyright © 1989 by the Division of Christian Education of the National
Council of the Churches of Christ in the USA.
Used by permission. All rights reserved.

ISBN 0-687-054478

Writer/Editor: LeeDell B. Stickler
Production Editor: Heidi Hewitt
Production and Design Manager: R.E. Osborne
Designer: Paige Easter
Cover Design: Paige Easter

Illustrators: Cover by Charles Jakubowski; pp. 6–13, 15–21, 23–24, 26–35, 37–63 by
Megan Jeffery; p. 5 by Susan Harrison; pp. 22, 25, 36 by Jim Padgett.

04 05 06 07 08 09 10 11 12 13—10 9 8 7 6 5 4 3 2 1
MANUFACTURED IN THE UNITED STATES OF AMERICA

TABLE OF CONTENTS

Old Testament

TITLE	CATEGORY	SCRIPTURE	PAGE
Out of Chaos	Creation	Genesis 1:1–5	5
On the Fourth Day	Creation	Genesis 1:14–19	6
Who Is It?	Creation	Genesis 1:11–13	7
Cross It Out!	Creation	Genesis 1:26–31	8
A Dire Warning	Creation	Genesis 2:15–17	9
Noah's Floating Zoo	Creation	Genesis 6:9–22	10
On the Move	Patriarchs	Genesis 12:1–9	11
Good News for Sarah	Patriarchs	Genesis 18:1–15	12
A Wife for Isaac	Patriarchs	Genesis 24:1–67	13
A Sneaky Trick	Patriarchs	Genesis 27	14
Jacob's Dream	Patriarchs	Genesis 28:10–22	15
Brothers Reunited	Patriarchs	Genesis 33:1–11	16
A Baby in a Basket	Moses	Exodus 2:1–10	17
The Big Mistake	Moses	Exodus 2:11–15	18
Let My People Go!	Moses	Exodus 5:1–12:41	19
Through the Sea	Moses	Exodus 14:1–31	20
Moses Mystery	Moses	Exodus 19:1–13	21
God's Top Ten	Moses	Exodus 20:1–19	22
Into the Promised Land	Joshua	Joshua 1:1–18	23
The Twelve Stones	Joshua	Joshua 4	24
The Falling Walls	Joshua	Joshua 6:1–20	25
With My Whole Heart	The Shema	Deuteronomy 6:4–9	26
David the Shepherd	David	1 Samuel 16:1–13	27
Elijah and the Widow	Elijah	1 Kings 17:8–16	28
The Many Jars of Oil	Elisha	2 Kings 4:1–7	29
Josiah and the Temple	Josiah	2 Kings 22:1–23:3	30
Psalm 23	Psalms	Psalm 23:1–3	31
Jonah and the Fish	Jonah	Jonah 1–3	32
The Messiah Is Coming	Isaiah	Isaiah 11:1–9	33
Jesse's Family Tree	Isaiah	Isaiah 11:1–5	34

TABLE OF CONTENTS
(CONTINUED)

New Testament

TITLE	CATEGORY	SCRIPTURE	PAGE
From the Line of David	Jesus' Birth	Matthew 1:1–17	35
Gabriel's Message	Jesus' Birth	Luke 1:26–38	36
Journey to Bethlehem	Jesus' Birth	Luke 2:1–7	37
His Name Will Be Jesus	Jesus' Birth	Luke 1:29–33	38
In a Stable	Jesus' Birth	Luke 2:1–7	39
John the Baptist	John the Baptist	Matthew 3:13–17	40
Following Jesus	Jesus' Ministry	Matthew 4:18–22	41
The First Disciples	Jesus' Ministry	Mark 1:16–20	42
Two-by-Two	Jesus' Ministry	Luke 9:1–6	43
A Stormy Day	Jesus' Ministry	Luke 8:22–25	44
Feeding 5,000	Jesus' Ministry	John 6:1–15	45
Jesus Heals	Jesus' Ministry	John 5:1–18	46
Jesus Teaches	Jesus' Ministry	Matthew 19:16–22	47
The Man in the Tree	Jesus' Ministry	Luke 19:1–10	48
Living in God's Kingdom	Jesus' Ministry	Matthew 5:1–12	49
A Tree and Its Fruit	Jesus' Ministry	Luke 6:27–45	50
The Good Samaritan	Jesus' Ministry	Luke 10:25–37	51
A New Commandment	Jesus' Ministry	John 13:31–35	52
A Story of Two Sons	Jesus' Ministry	Luke 15:11–32	53
Two Builders	Jesus' Ministry	Matthew 7:24–29	54
Hosanna!	Holy Week	Mark 11:1–11	55
The Last Supper	Holy Week	Mark 14:22–25	56
I Don't Know Him!	Holy Week	Luke 22:54–62	57
Symbols of Easter	Easter	Matthew 28:1–10	58
Breakfast on the Beach	After Easter	John 21:1–14	59
A Love Letter	Paul	1 Corinthians 13:1–13	60
Lydia	Paul	Acts 16:11–15	61
Fruits of the Spirit	Paul	Galatians 5:22–26	62
Living the Word	Christian Living		63
Answers			64

DIG INTO THE BIBLE

OUT OF CHAOS

In the beginning the universe was a formless void.
Out of this chaos God created all that is.
Can you find the words to the Bible verse below in the swirling chaos?

As soon as God spoke the world was created; at his command, the
earth was formed. (Psalm 33:9, CEV, adapted)

GENESIS 1:1–5

DIG INTO THE BIBLE

ON THE FOURTH DAY

Answers on: pg. 64

On the first day of creation, God created light and dark.
On the second and third days, God created the sky, the seas, and the earth.
Use the letter/number squares to find what God created on the fourth day.

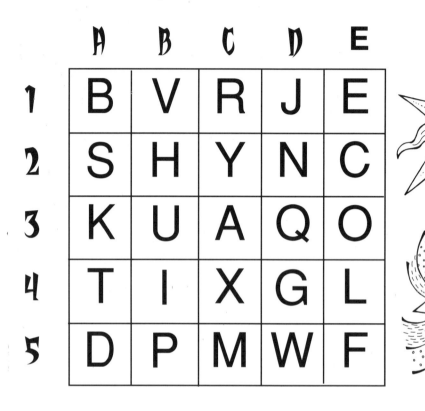

	A	B	C	D	E
1	B	V	R	J	E
2	S	H	Y	N	C
3	K	U	A	Q	O
4	T	I	X	G	L
5	D	P	M	W	F

_____

D4 E3 A5   C5 C3 A5 E1   A4 D5 E3

_____

D4 C1 E1 C3 A4   E4 B4 D4 B2 A4 A2

_____

C3 D2 A5   A4 B2 E1   A2 A4 C3 C1 A2

GENESIS 1:14-19

DIG INTO THE BIBLE

WHO IS IT?

Answers on: pg. 64

Who commanded the earth to produce all kinds of vegetation?
Color those spaces marked with a star red to discover the answer.
Color all the other spaces blue.

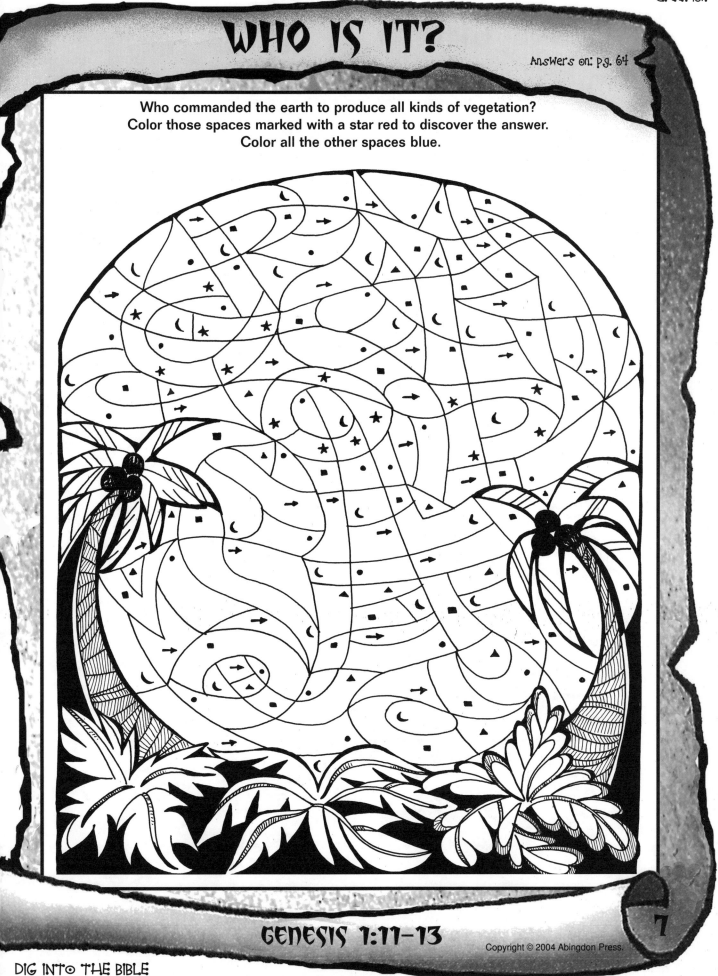

GENESIS 1:11–13

CROSS IT OUT!

Answers on: pg. 64

On the sixth day, God created human beings.
God created humans in his own image. Cross out all the X's.
Cross out all the Z's. Cross out all the Q's. What words tell us about God?

```
K Z C F P X G F D X
X L Z A A Z X Z E Q
Q O A I X Q X A P Z
Z X R R Z X O I E Z
I Q X S T R O X N G
Q V I X I Q Z T D X
Z I N X Q Z Z H A Q
N Z Q Q E X D F B Z
X N G Q N Q X U L Q
D G E N T Z Q L E X
```

GENESIS 1:26–31

DIG INTO THE BIBLE

A DIRE WARNING

Answers on: pg. 64

God created a wonderful garden and placed Adam and Eve in it.
God told them they could eat of anything in that garden except what?
Starting at the star, connect the dots to discover the answer.

GENESIS 2:15-17

DIG INTO THE BIBLE

NOAH'S FLOATING ZOO

Answers on: pg. 64

God caused a great flood to cover the earth.
God had Noah build a giant boat to save two of each kind of animal.
How many animals can you find in the word puzzle?

```
A N T E L O P E X R
C A M E L G O A T A
Z O S T R I C H U B
B W Z B I R D Q R B
E L E P H A N T T I
A I B S A F D I L T
R O R H W F O G E P
E N A E K E G E E I
M Z B E A V E R L G
U Q X P D O N K E Y
```

GENESIS 6:9–22

DIG INTO THE BIBLE

ON THE MOVE

Answers on: pg. 64

God promised to lead Abraham and Sarah to a special land.
They had to pack up everything they owned and follow God.
Can you help Jeremy pack up all of his things alphabetically?

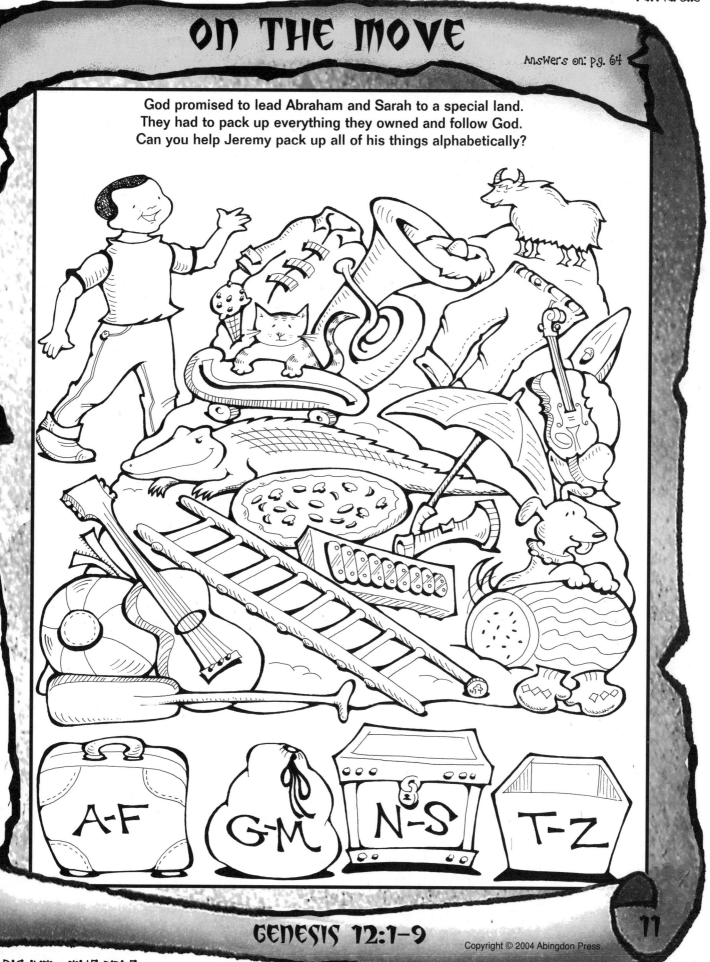

A-F   G-M   N-S   T-Z

GENESIS 12:1–9

DIG INTO THE BIBLE

GOOD NEWS FOR SARAH

Answers on: pg. 64

God promised Abraham that one day he would be the father of a great nation.
One day three strangers came to Abraham's tent. They had good news for Abraham.
Unscramble each word.

One day Abraham saw three _____ (nme)

standing near his _____ (ntte).

Abraham bowed down to the _____ (gdrnou).

He brought them _____ (oodf) and

_____(trawe). The men told

_____(habraam) that he and Sarah

would soon have a _____(dlich), even though

she and Abraham were very _____ (dol).

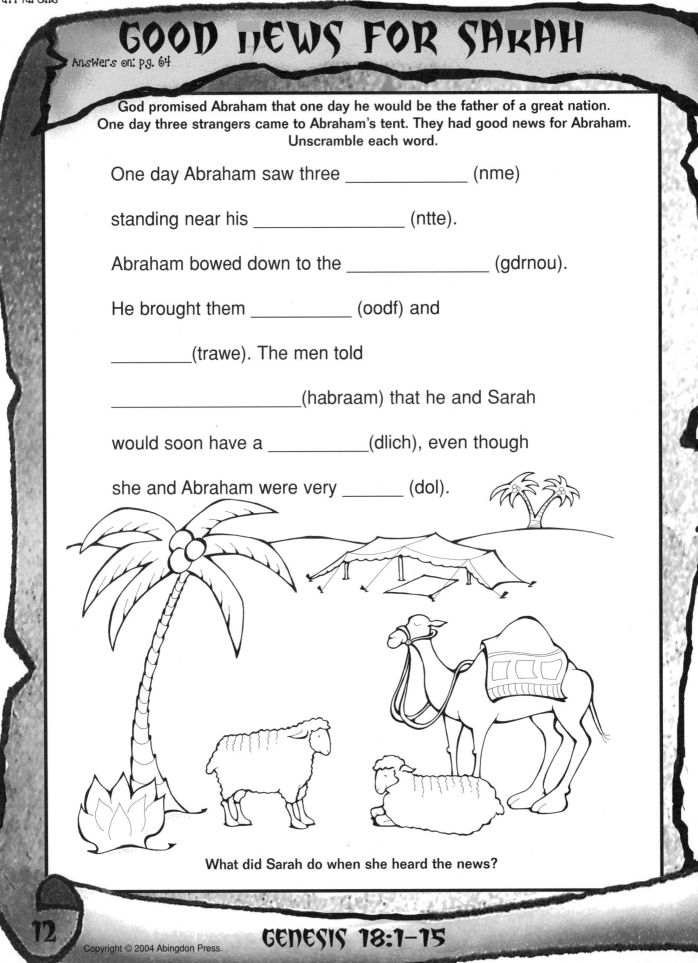

What did Sarah do when she heard the news?

GENESIS 18:1-15

DIG INTO THE BIBLE

A WIFE FOR ISAAC

Answers on: pg. 64

**When Abraham's son Isaac became old enough,
Abraham decided to find a wife for him. Look up the Bible story.
Using the words in the box, complete the story.**

(1) _____ sent his (2) _____

to (3) _____ to find a wife for (4) _____.

The servant took (5) _____ of his master's (6) _____

with him. The servant waited by the (7) _____ until the women

came to get (8) _____. (9) _____

offered to get water for the servant and his camels. The servant gave

Rebekah a (10) _____ and bracelets. He offered her

family (11) _____ of gold and silver. Rebekah agreed to go back

to Canaan and become Isaac's (12) _____.

Word Box
water, ten,
camels,
Abraham,
Rebekah,
gifts, wife,
ring, well,
Isaac,
servant,
Nahor

GENESIS 24:1–67

DIG INTO THE BIBLE

A SNEAKY TRICK

Answers on: pg. 64

Isaac was old and nearly blind.
It was easy for Jacob to fool him into giving Jacob Esau's blessing.
Use the Braille** alphabet. What did Jacob learn?

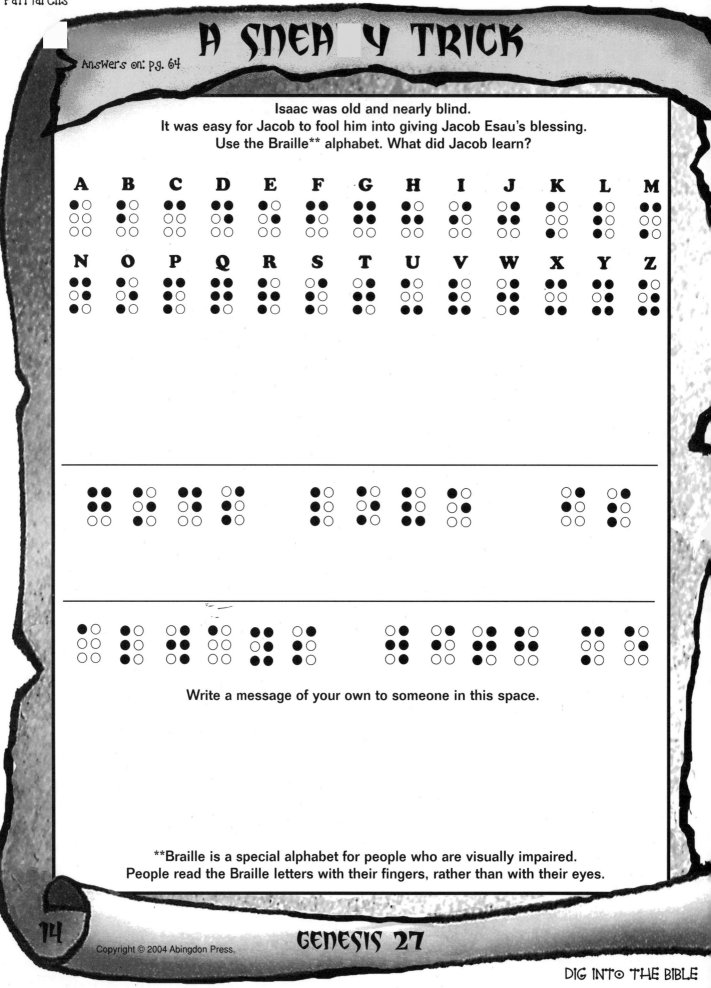

Write a message of your own to someone in this space.

**Braille is a special alphabet for people who are visually impaired.
People read the Braille letters with their fingers, rather than with their eyes.

GENESIS 27

DIG INTO THE BIBLE

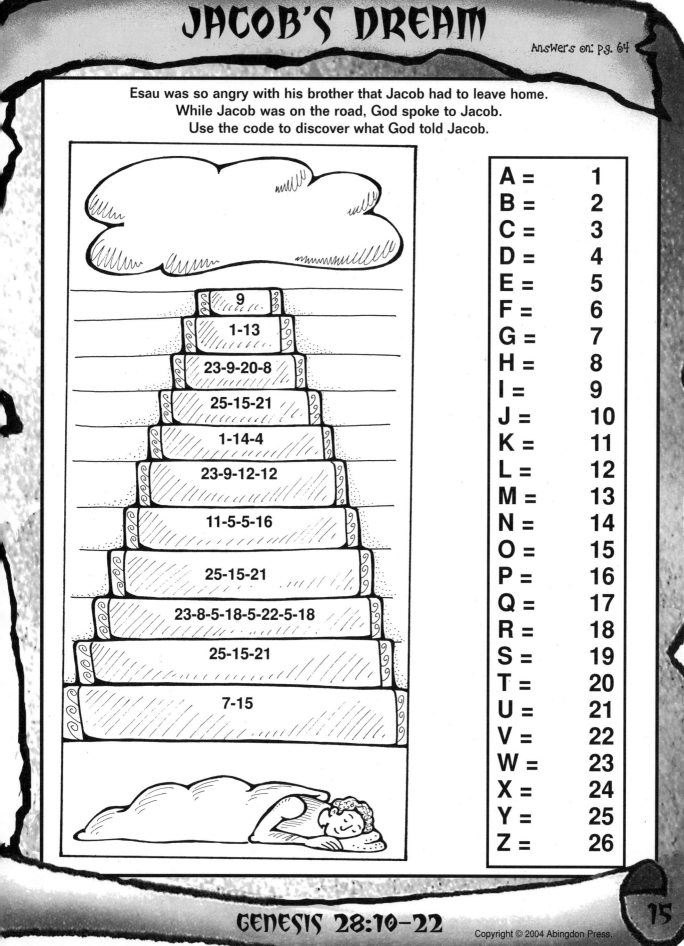

JACOB'S DREAM

Answers on: pg. 64

Esau was so angry with his brother that Jacob had to leave home.
While Jacob was on the road, God spoke to Jacob.
Use the code to discover what God told Jacob.

9

1-13

23-9-20-8

25-15-21

1-14-4

23-9-12-12

11-5-5-16

25-15-21

23-8-5-18-5-22-5-18

25-15-21

7-15

A =	1
B =	2
C =	3
D =	4
E =	5
F =	6
G =	7
H =	8
I =	9
J =	10
K =	11
L =	12
M =	13
N =	14
O =	15
P =	16
Q =	17
R =	18
S =	19
T =	20
U =	21
V =	22
W =	23
X =	24
Y =	25
Z =	26

GENESIS 28:10-22

DIG INTO THE BIBLE

BROTHERS REUNITED

Answers on: pg. 64

Jacob lived in Haran for a long, long time. Then one day, God told
Jacob it was time to go back home. Jacob was afraid of what Esau might do.
Follow the maze. What gift did Esau offer his brother?

GENESIS 33:1–11

DIG INTO THE BIBLE

A BABY IN A BASKET

Answers on: pg. 64

Use the letter cube to discover the answer to this question.
Why did the princess call the baby "Moses"?

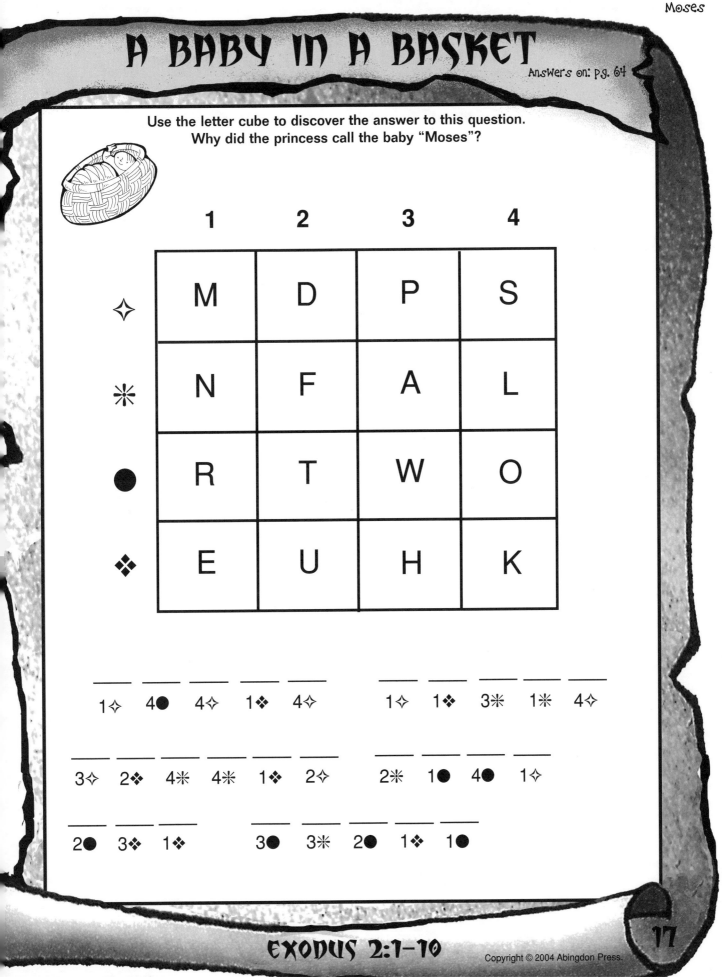

	1	2	3	4
✧	M	D	P	S
❋	N	F	A	L
●	R	T	W	O
❖	E	U	H	K

___ ___ ___ ___ ___   ___ ___ ___ ___ ___
1✧ 4● 4✧ 1❖ 4✧   1✧ 1❖ 3❋ 1❋ 4✧

___ ___ ___ ___ ___ ___   ___ ___ ___ ___
3✧ 2❖ 4❋ 4❋ 1❖ 2✧   2❋ 1● 4● 1✧

___ ___ ___   ___ ___ ___ ___ ___
2● 3❖ 1❖   3● 3❋ 2● 1❖ 1●

EXODUS 2:1–10

DIG INTO THE BIBLE

THE BIG MISTAKE

Answers on: pg. 64

When Moses killed the Egyptian overseer and ran away,
it was a big mistake. Look at the picture here.
How many mistakes can you find?

EXODUS 2:11–15

DIG INTO THE BIBLE

LET MY PEOPLE GO!

God sent these animals to upset the Egyptians
and make the Pharaoh let the Hebrew people leave.
Color all the spaces with a dot green. Color all the spaces with an X blue.

EXODUS 5:1–12:41

DIG INTO THE BIBLE

THROUGH THE SEA

Answers on: pg. 64

God rescued the Hebrew people by making a dry path for them through the sea. What did the Egyptians learn? Draw a path through the puzzle. Start at the arrow. You may move up, down, or side to side, but not diagonally. Check Exodus 14:25.

EXODUS 14:1-31

DIG INTO THE BIBLE

MOSES MYSTERY

Answers on: pg. 64

What is this special place? To solve the mystery,
color every dot red or orange and every X brown or black.

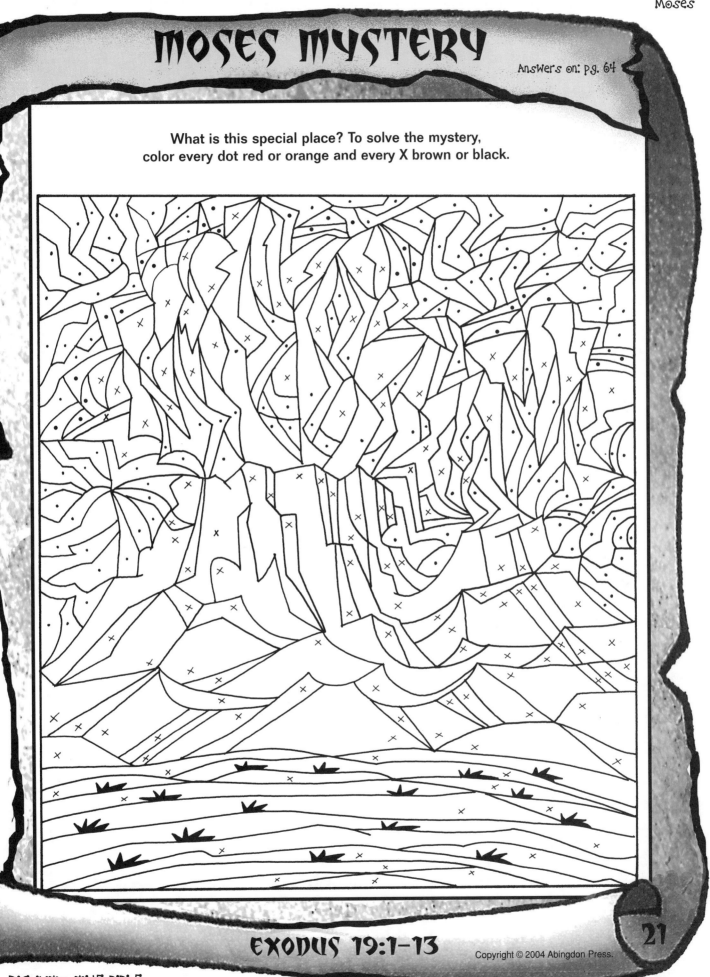

EXODUS 19:1–13

DIG INTO THE BIBLE

GOD'S TOP TEN

Answers on: pg. 64

God gave the people ten rules to live by.
Can you match the halves of each commandment?

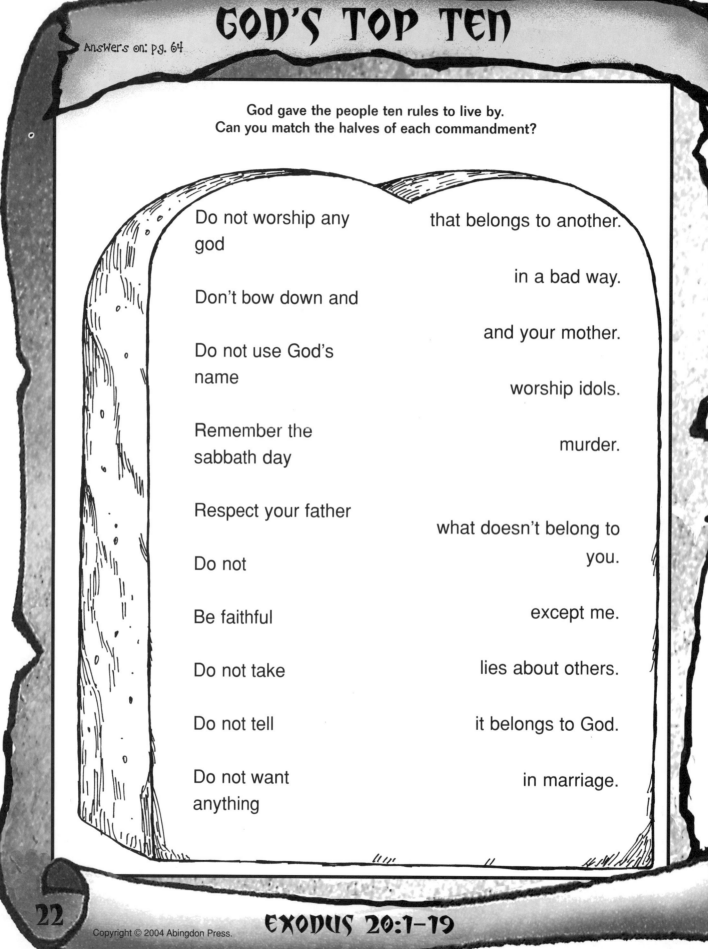

Do not worship any god

that belongs to another.

in a bad way.

Don't bow down and

and your mother.

Do not use God's name

worship idols.

Remember the sabbath day

murder.

Respect your father

what doesn't belong to you.

Do not

except me.

Be faithful

Do not take

lies about others.

Do not tell

it belongs to God.

Do not want anything

in marriage.

EXODUS 20:1-19

DIG INTO THE BIBLE

INTO THE PROMISED LAND

For forty years, God led the Hebrew people.
They were going to the land of milk and honey.
Can you help the people find the Promised Land?

JOSHUA 1:1-18

DIG INTO THE BIBLE

THE TWELVE STONES

Answers on: pg. 64

When Joshua and the people of Israel crossed the Jordan River,
they built a memorial from twelve stones.
What would the stones remind them to do?

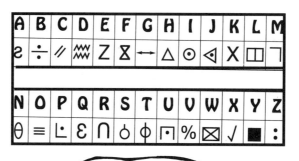

JOSHUA 4

DIG INTO THE BIBLE

THE FALLING WALLS

Answers on: pg. 64

God's people came to the Promised Land. But the city of Jericho stood in the way.
God had a plan if Joshua would only do as God said.
Use the box of words to fill in the missing words.

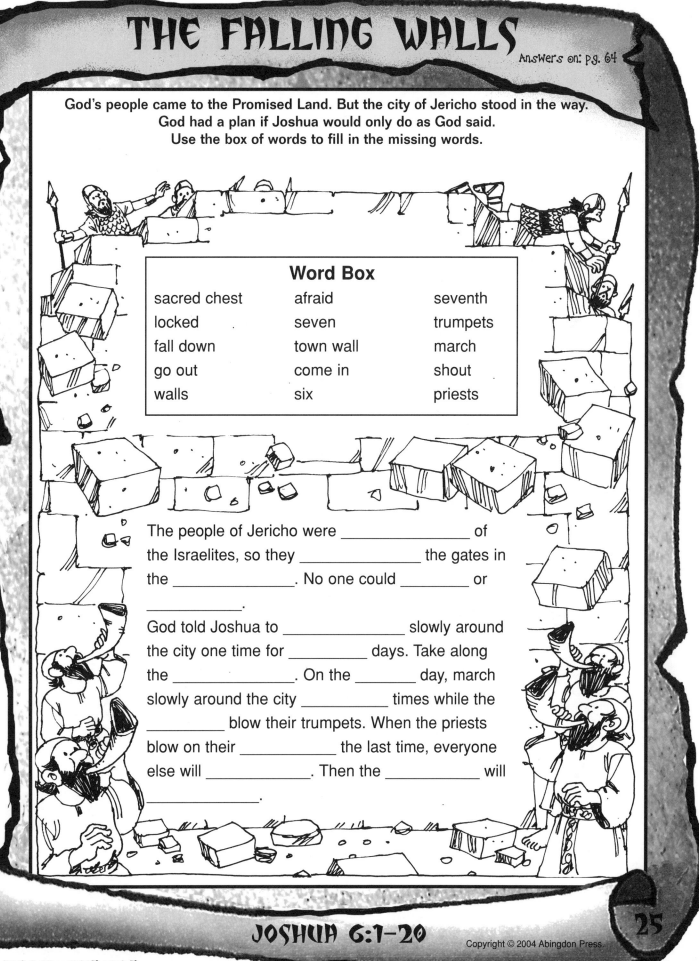

Word Box

sacred chest	afraid	seventh
locked	seven	trumpets
fall down	town wall	march
go out	come in	shout
walls	six	priests

The people of Jericho were _____ of the Israelites, so they _____ the gates in the _____. No one could _____ or _____.

God told Joshua to _____ slowly around the city one time for _____ days. Take along the _____. On the _____ day, march slowly around the city _____ times while the _____ blow their trumpets. When the priests blow on their _____ the last time, everyone else will _____. Then the _____ will _____.

WITH MY WHOLE HEART

The Bible tells us to love God with all our heart, with all our soul, and with all our might. Finish the design on each heart so that both sides match.

DEUTERONOMY 6:4-9

DIG INTO THE BIBLE

DAVID THE SHEPHERD

When Samuel came to Bethlehem to anoint a new king,
Jesse's son David was in the field watching the sheep.
Look at the picture. Can you find the items listed below?

As a shepherd, David would have to be very watchful to keep his sheep safe.
Look at the picture. Can you find these things: 4 butterflies, 2 caterpillars,
1 baby lamb, 1 nest of baby birds, 3 rabbits, 2 frogs, 3 mice, 2 turtles,
2 ladybugs, 1 cloud, and 10 flowers?

1 SAMUEL 16:1-13

DIG INTO THE BIBLE

Elijah

ELIJAH AND THE WIDOW

Answers on: pg. 64

Elijah was a prophet of God. During the drought, God sent ravens to bring Elijah bread and meat. Then God sent Elijah to stay with a widow. Because she helped him, Elijah gave her a special gift. What was it?

H ____ ____   j ____ ____ S   **A**

____ ____ ____ i ____   **R**

____ ____ d   **L**

____ ____ ____ u ____   **O**

W ____ ____ ____   **E**

____ ____ v ____ ____   **N**

____ m p t y.   **F**

1 KINGS 17:8–16

DIG INTO THE BIBLE

THE MANY JARS OF OIL

Elisha helped a widow by causing her small jar of olive oil to fill many jars. She sold the oil and paid off her debts. Look at the many jars. Can you find the ones that exactly match?

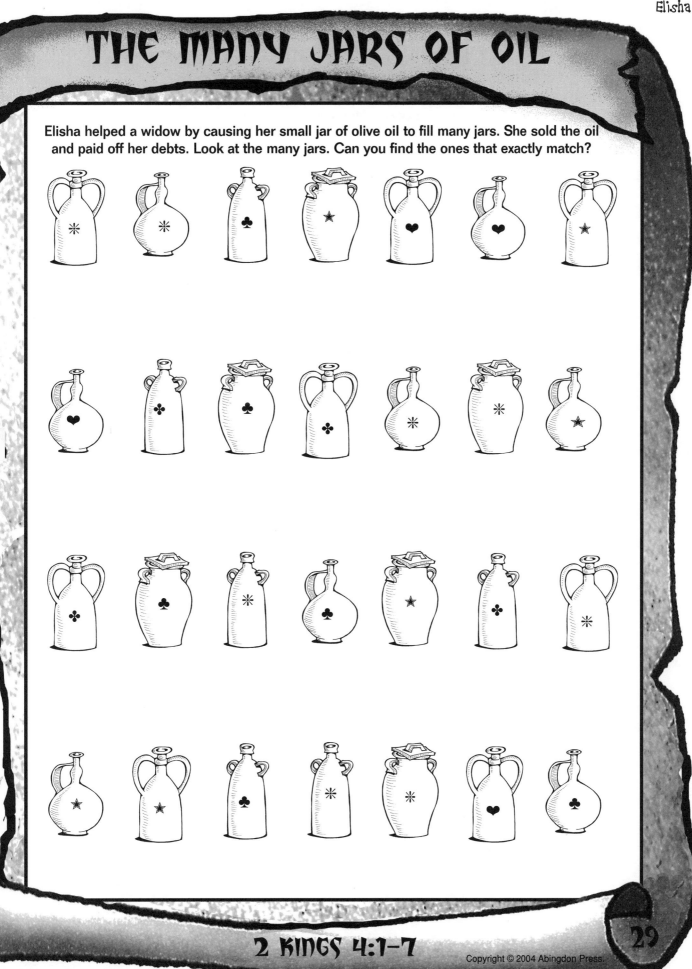

2 KINGS 4:1-7

DIG INTO THE BIBLE

JOSIAH AND THE TEMPLE

Answers on: pg. 64

Josiah became king when he was only a boy.
When he grew older, Josiah decided to restore the Temple. What did the workers find?
Mark out all the X's, Q's, Z's, P's, and S's

X	S	Z	Q	S	P
Q	B	X	P	S	P
S	P	O	Z	Q	Z
Z	Q	S	O	Q	X
Q	P	Q	Z	K	P
Z	T	Q	O	P	S
S	Z	H	Q	F	S
P	Q	S	E	P	X
Z	P	Q	X	P	Z
P	L	X	Z	S	P
Q	X	A	S	P	Q
S	P	Z	W	Q	Z
Z	Q	P	X	P	X
					S

2 KINGS 22:1–23:3

DIG INTO THE BIBLE

PSALM 23

Use the picture code to fill in the missing letters of the psalm.
David says that God is like a shepherd.
What does that mean for us?

Th_ L_RD _s my sh_ph_rd,
■ ◆ ▲ ■ ■

_ sh_ll n_t w_nt.
▲ ● ◆ ●

H_ m_k_s m_ l__ d_wn
■ ● ■ ■ ▲ ■ ◆

_n gr__n p_stur_s;
▲ ■ ■ ● ■

h_ l__ds m_
■ ■ ● ■

b_s_d_
■ ▲ ■

st_ll w_t_rs;
▲ ● ■

h_
■

r_st_r_s
■ ◆ ■

my s_u l.
◆

● = a
■ = e
▲ = i
◆ = o

PSALM 23:1-3

DIG INTO THE BIBLE

JONAH AND THE FISH

God caused Jonah to be swallowed by a great fish.
From the belly of the fish, Jonah prayed to God.
Then the fish spit Jonah out onto dry land. Help Jonah find his way out.

JONAH 1–3

DIG INTO THE BIBLE

THE MESSIAH IS COMING

Answers on: pg. 64

The prophet Isaiah said that when the promised Messiah came, even the animals that were enemies would live together in this way. Color the ■ red. Color the ✕ blue. Color the ★ green, Color the ▲ purple. Color the ● yellow. Color the — orange.

ISAIAH 11:1-9

Copyright © 2004 Abingdon Press.

DIG INTO THE BIBLE

JESSE'S FAMILY TREE

The prophet Isaiah said that the Messiah would come from the family of Jesse.
Each of the symbols stands for a person.
Can you find the symbols on Jesse's tree?

ISAIAH 11:1–5

DIG INTO THE BIBLE

FROM THE LINE OF DAVID

The prophets said that the Messiah would come from the line of David. Joseph came from the line of King David. Use the beginning letter on each leaf to choose one of Jesus' relatives to write on the tree.

MATTHEW 1:1–17

DIG INTO THE BIBLE

GABRIEL'S MESSAGE

Answers on: pg. 64

God sent the angel Gabriel to the town of Nazareth with a message for a young girl named Mary. Mark out all the X's, Q's, Z's and K's. What was the message the angel delivered?

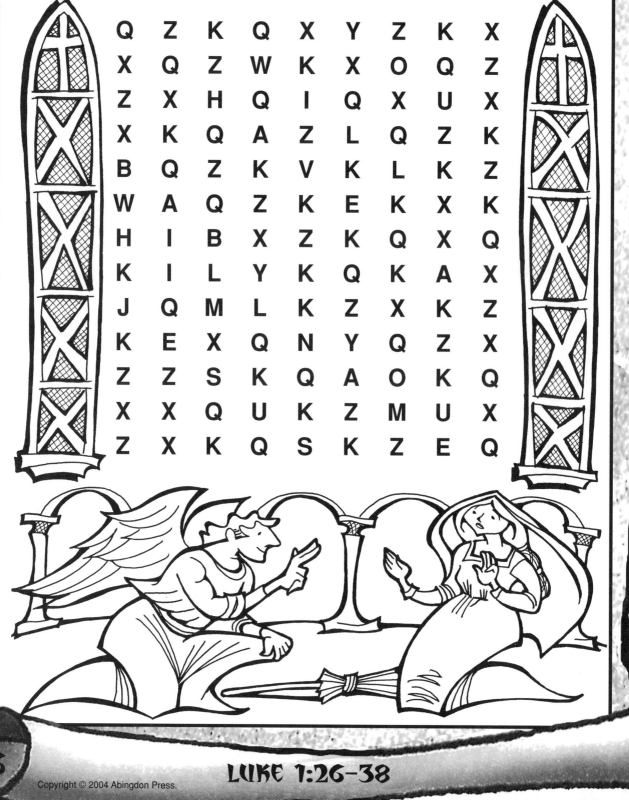

```
Q  Z  K  Q  X  Y  Z  K  X
X  Q  Z  W  K  X  O  Q  Z
Z  X  H  Q  I  Q  X  U  X
X  K  Q  A  Z  L  Q  Z  K
B  Q  Z  K  V  K  L  K  Z
W  A  Q  Z  K  E  K  X  K
H  I  B  X  Z  K  Q  X  Q
K  I  L  Y  K  Q  K  A  X
J  Q  M  L  K  Z  X  K  Z
K  E  X  Q  N  Y  Q  Z  X
Z  Z  S  K  Q  A  O  K  Q
X  X  Q  U  K  Z  M  U  X
Z  X  K  Q  S  K  Z  E  Q
```

LUKE 1:26-38

DIG INTO THE BIBLE

JOURNEY TO BETHLEHEM

Answers on: pg. 64

Why did Mary and Joseph travel to Bethlehem?
Use the special code to discover the answer.

Code Box

A = 1	B = 2	C = 3
D = 4	E = 5	F = 6
G = 7	H = 8	I = 9
L = 10	M = 11	N = 12
O = 13	P = 14	R = 15
S = 16	T = 17	U = 18
W = 19		

1 4 5 3 15 5 5   19 5 12 17   13 18 17   6 15 13 11

5 11 14 5 15 13 15

1 18 7 18 16 17 18 16   17 8 1 17

1 10 10   17 8 5   19 13 15 10 4   16 8 13 18 10 4

2 5   15 5 7 9 16 17 5 15 5 4

LUKE 2:1-7

37

DIG INTO THE BIBLE

HIS NAME WILL BE JESUS

Answers on: pg. 64

During Jesus' life he was known by many different names.
Mary and Joseph called him Jesus. What are some of his other names?
Use the Scripture references to help you out.

_____ (Matthew 1:23)

_____ (Matthew 2:2)

_____ (John 1:38)

_____ (Mark 10:47)

_____ (John 10:11)

_____ (Luke 1:32)

_____ (Luke 2:11)

_____ (John 1:29)

_____ (Matthew 16:16)

Good Shepherd, Son of David, King of the
Jews, Rabbi, Emmanuel, Savior, Son of the
Most High, Lamb of God, Messiah

LUKE 1:29-33

DIG INTO THE BIBLE

IN A STABLE

Answers on: pg. 64

Cut out the picture squares on the dark lines.
Then arrange the squares to form a picture. Where was baby Jesus born?

LUKE 2:1-7

DIG INTO THE BIBLE

JOHN THE BAPTIST

Answers on: pg. 64

When John baptized Jesus in the Jordan River,
he saw a dove and heard a voice. Mark out all the X's.
Mark out all the Z's. Mark out all the Q's. What did the voice say?

```
X  Y  Q  Z  X  O  Q  Z  Q  U
A  X  Q  R  Q  Z  E  X  Q  Z
Z  Q  M  X  Z  Q  X  X  Q  Y
S  Z  Q  X  O  Z  Q  N  Z  Q
X  Q  T  Q  Z  H  Z  X  Q  E
B  E  Q  L  O  Z  V  X  E  D
Z  W  I  X  Q  Z  X  T  H  X
Y  Q  O  Z  X  U  X  Q  I  Z
A  M  X  Q  Z  W  E  X  L  L
Z  P  L  X  E  A  Q  S  E  D
```

ANSWER BOX:

MATTHEW 3:13-17

DIG INTO THE BIBLE

FOLLOWING JESUS

Answers on: pg. 64

Jesus called Peter and Andrew to follow him.
They left their nets and their boats behind.
But where are all the fish? How many can you find?

MATTHEW 4:18-22

DIG INTO THE BIBLE

THE FIRST DISCIPLES

Answers on: pg. 64

Cut out the picture squares on the dark lines.
Then arrange the squares to form a picture.
What did Peter, Andrew, James, and John do for a living?

MARK 1:16-20

DIG INTO THE BIBLE

TWO-BY-TWO

Answers on: pg. 64

Jesus sent his disciples out in pairs to tell others about the Kingdom of God.
Can you find the pairs of fish in this aquarium?

Stumper:
What could the disciples take with
them on their trip?
Look up Luke 9:3.

LUKE 9:1-6

DIG INTO THE BIBLE

A STORMY DAY

Answers on: pg. 64

One day while Jesus and the disciples were out in a boat on Lake Galilee,
a great storm came up. Look at the picture.
How many different kinds of boats can you find?

LUKE 8:22–25

DIG INTO THE BIBLE

FEEDING 5,000

One day Jesus fed a crowd of five thousand with one small boy's lunch.
Can you find the five loaves of bread and two fish that Jesus used?

JOHN 6:1–15

DIG INTO THE BIBLE

Jesus' Ministry

JESUS HEALS

Answers on: pg. 64

Many people who were sick or blind came to Jesus to be healed.
One day Jesus came across a man who had been sick for thirty-eight years.
What did Jesus tell him?

	1	2	3	4
♠	P	A	U	K
♦	M	C	Y	T
♣	O	L	N	R
♥	D	B	W	I

___ ___ ___ ___   ___ ___
1♠ 4♥ 2♦ 4♠   3♠ 1♠

___ ___ ___ ___   ___ ___ ___
3♦ 1♣ 3♠ 4♣   1♦ 2♠ 4♦

___ ___ ___   ___ ___ ___ ___
2♠ 3♣ 1♥   3♥ 2♠ 2♣ 4♠

JOHN 5:1-18

Copyright © 2004 Abingdon Press.

DIG INTO THE BIBLE

JESUS TEACHES

Answers on: pg. 64

A rich young man once asked Jesus what he must do to have eternal life.
Jesus told him to love God and to love his neighbor.
How many hearts can you find in the picture?

MATTHEW 19:16–22

DIG INTO THE BIBLE

THE MAN IN THE TREE

Answers on: pg. 64

**Read the story of Zacchaeus from your Bible.
Then fill in the missing words.
Choose from the Word Box below.**

Jesus was going through _____.

There lived a man named _____.

He was a _____.

Zacchaeus was a _____ man.

In order to see Jesus, he climbed up in a _____ tree.

When Jesus saw him, he told him to come _____.

Jesus was going to his house for _____.

Zacchaeus said that he would give _____ of his property to the poor.

Zacchaeus said that he would pay back _____ times the people he had _____.

Jesus told Zacchaeus, "Today you and your family have been _____."

Word Box
saved, short, half, four, cheated, dinner, sycamore, Jericho, down, tax collector, Zacchaeus

48

LUKE 19:1-10

LIVING IN GOD'S KINGDOM

Answers on: pg. 64

Jesus taught the people what it would be like to live in God's kingdom.
Start with each car. Then follow the road to the box below You will go over and under.
Who does God bless?

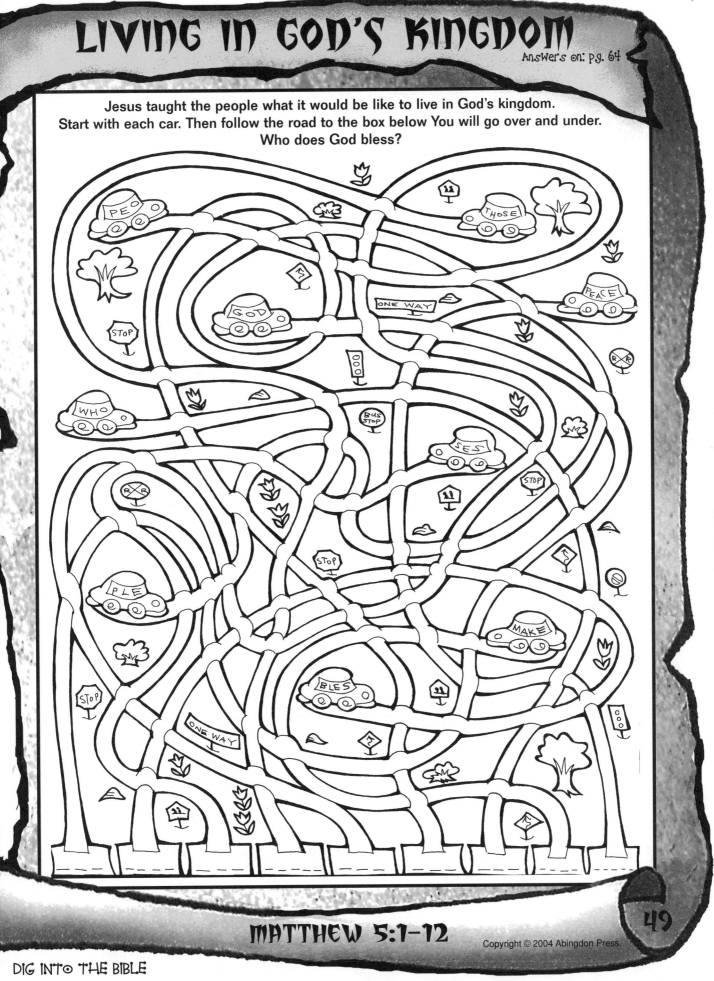

MATTHEW 5:1-12

DIG INTO THE BIBLE

49

A TREE AND ITS FRUIT

Answers on: pg. 64

Use your Bible to help you fill in the missing words.
Then color the fruit as the baskets tell you.

forgiven

judge

you

yell

others

good

beat

no one

love

hate

No (red) tree bears bad fruit. Luke 6:43

(yellow) your enemies. Luke 6:27

Do not (purple) and you will not be judged. Luke 6:37

Forgive, and you will be (blue) Luke 6:37

Do to (orange) as you would have them do to you. Luke 6:31

LUKE 6:27-45

DIG INTO THE BIBLE

THE GOOD SAMARITAN

Answers on: pg. 64

Jesus told a story about a good Samaritan
who helped an injured traveler.
What did the story tell people to do? Starting with the L, circle every other letter.

LAOCVEEFYGOHUIRJNKELIMGN

HOBPOQRRASSTYVOWUXLYOZV

BEAYBOCUDRESFEBLDFB

LUKE 10:25-37

Copyright © 2004 Abingdon Press.

DIG INTO THE BIBLE

A NEW COMMANDMENT

Answers on: pg. 64

Jesus gave his disciples a new commandment.
Use the signal flags to discover what it was.

Anchors Away!

JOHN 13:31-35

DIG INTO THE BIBLE

A STORY OF TWO SONS

Answers on: pg. 64

Jesus told stories called parables to help people understand what God was like.
Fill in the missing words. Then take the letters in circles and unscramble
them to discover what we learn about God from this story.

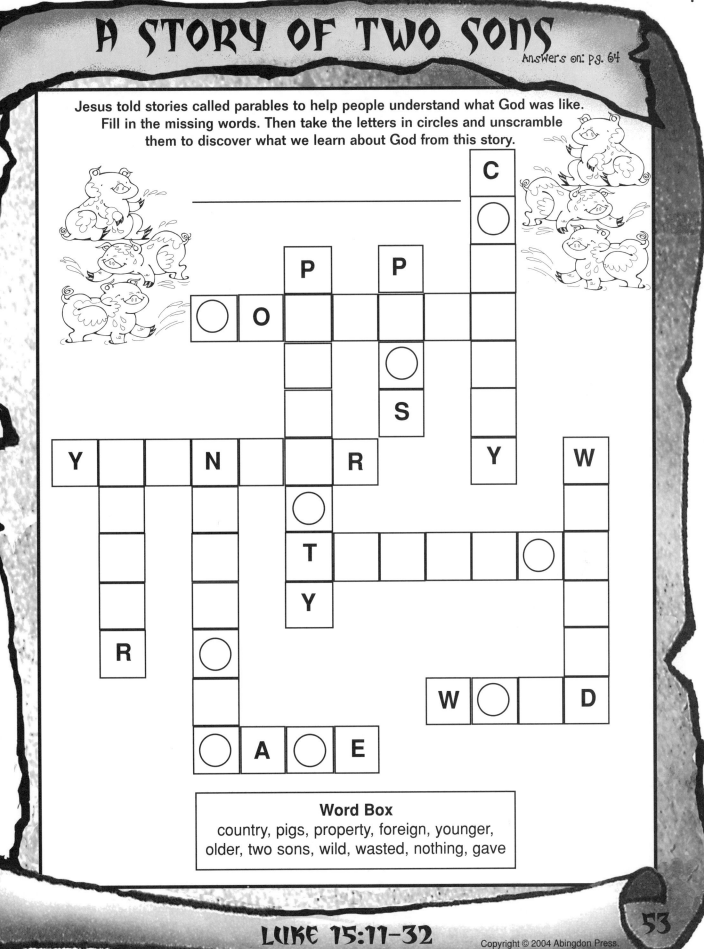

Word Box
country, pigs, property, foreign, younger,
older, two sons, wild, wasted, nothing, gave

LUKE 15:11–32

Copyright © 2004 Abingdon Press.

DIG INTO THE BIBLE

TWO BUILDERS

Answers on: pg. 64

Jesus told a story about two builders—
one who built a house on a solid foundation, one who built a house on sand.
What did this story teach the people? Use the code to discover the answer.

A = 26   B = 25   C = 24   D = 23   E = 22   F = 21   G = 20   H = 19   I = 18

J = 17   K = 16   L = 15   M = 14   N = 13   O = 12   P = 11   Q = 10   R = 9

S = 8   T = 7   U = 6   V = 5   W = 4   X = 3   Y = 2   Z = 1

11 22 12 11 15 22   4 19 12   15 18 8 7 22 13

7 12   17 22 8 6 8   7 22 26 24 19 18 13 20 8

26 13 23   12 25 22 2   7 19 22 14

26 9 22   4 18 8 22

MATTHEW 7:24-29

DIG INTO THE BIBLE

HOSANNA!

Answers on: pg. 64

Jesus and his disciples came to Jerusalem to celebrate the Passover.
People greeted him with palm branches and loud "Hosannas!"
What do we call this special Sunday? Find the letters on the road.

MARK 11:1-11

DIG INTO THE BIBLE

THE LAST SUPPER

Answers on: pg. 64

At the Last Supper, Jesus gave his disciples a new way to remember him. Today we remember Jesus at church in a special way. Mark out all the X's. Mark out all the Z's. Mark out all the Q's. Mark out all the J's. What do we call this special time?

```
C X Z Q H J X J Z X
X O Q J X O J Q X Q
Q J M X J Q L X J X
J X Q M X J Q Y J X
Q J X Q U J J X Z X
Z J Q X Z N Z Q J X
J X Z Q X J I Z X Z
Z Q X J X Z Q O Z X
X Z J X Q X Z X N Q
J X Q J X Z Q X Z X
```

MARK 14:22–25

DIG INTO THE BIBLE

I DON'T KNOW HIM!

At the Last Supper, Peter promised to always be there for Jesus.
But later that night he denied even knowing Jesus.
What animal reminded Peter that he had let his friend down? Use the color code.

1=red   2=green   3=brown   4=yellow   5=orange   6=blue

LUKE 22:54–62

DIG INTO THE BIBLE

SYMBOLS OF EASTER

Answers on: pg. 64

There are many symbols of Easter.
They remind us of something the women discovered that morning at the tomb.
Use the symbol code to discover the answer.

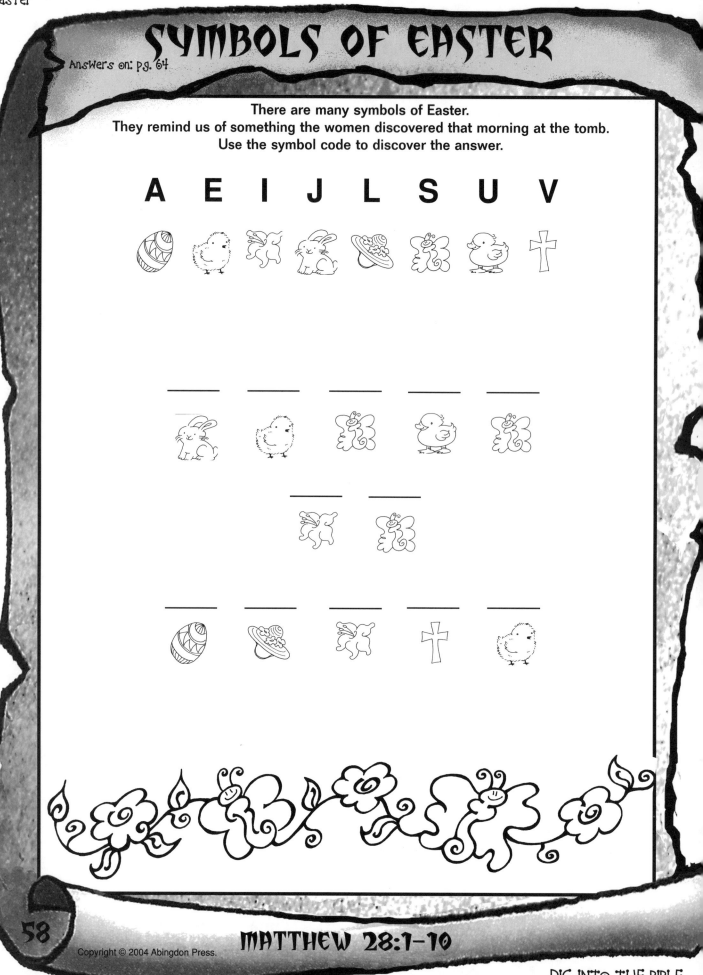

A   E   I   J   L   S   U   V

MATTHEW 28:1-10

DIG INTO THE BIBLE

BREAKFAST ON THE BEACH

Answers on: pg. 64

**Read the story of Jesus' appearance to his disciples.
Then number the statements in the correct order.**

☐ Then they knew that this was Jesus.

☐ They went out in the boat but didn't catch a thing that night.

☐ They caught so many fish that the boat almost sank.

☐ Simon Peter and some of the other disciples decided to go fishing.

☐ Peter recognized the man as Jesus.

☐ Peter jumped out of the boat and ran toward his friend Jesus.

☐ When the disciples got the boat on shore, Jesus had built a fire and was cooking some fish.

☐ When the disciples counted the number of fish they had caught, it was 153.

☐ Jesus told them, "Let your net down on the right side of your boat."

☐ Jesus took the bread in his hands and gave it to the disciples.

☐ The disciples said they had not caught a thing.

☐ The next morning, Jesus stood on the shore and asked, "Did you catch anything?"

JOHN 21:1–14

DIG INTO THE BIBLE

A LOVE LETTER

Paul became a follower of Jesus. He traveled around telling the good news about Jesus. In one of his letters, he told the church in Corinth what it meant to love. Can you find all the words that tell what love is?

```
N J S A N X Q K L O
E W U L O Y A L O T
V K P A T I E N T H
E I P J P J Z Z E E
R N O T R U D E S R
F D R L O V E S A S
A B T R U S T I N G
I Q I Q D N O T X A
L X V S E L F I S H
S Z E H O P E F U L
```

patient, kind, not proud, not rude,
not selfish, supportive, loyal,
hopeful, trusting, never fails

1 CORINTHIANS 13:1-13

DIG INTO THE BIBLE

LYDIA

Answers on: pg. 64

Lydia was a wealthy cloth merchant in Philippi.
When Paul told her about Jesus, she became a follower.
Use the code to discover why Paul and Silas came to Philippi.

ACTS 16:11–15

DIG INTO THE BIBLE

FRUITS OF THE SPIRIT

Answers on: pg. 64

In Paul's letter to the church at Galatia,
he told them how God's Spirit changes everyone. What are the fruits of the Spirit?
Use the fruit code to discover what people become.

A (apple)

E (banana)

I (orange)

L (strawberry)

N (pear)

O (lemon)

P (grapes)

T (pineapple)

___ ___ v ___ ___ g

H ___ ___ ___ y

___ ___ c ___ f u ___

___ ___ ___ ___ ___ ___ ___ ___

k ___ ___ d   g ___ ___ d

f ___ ___ ___ h f u ___

g ___ ___ ___ ___ ___

s ___ ___ f - c ___ ___ ___ ___ r ___ ___ ___ ___ d

GALATIANS 5:22-26

DIG INTO THE BIBLE

LIVING THE WORD

Answers on: pg. 64

The Bible teaches people how God wants us to live and to treat one another.
Sometimes the Bible teachings are different from what we expect.
Look at the picture. Circle any items that are different from what you might expect.

DIG INTO THE BIBLE

63

ANSWERS

Page 5: As soon as God spoke the world was created; at his command, the earth was formed.

Page 6: God made two great lights and the stars.

Page 7: God

Page 8: Down—kind, loving, caring, fair, patient, good, faithful, dependable; Across—strong, gentle

Page 9: the tree at the center of the garden

Page 10: Across—ant, antelope, camel, goat, ostrich, bird, elephant, beaver, donkey; Down—bear, emu, owl, lion, zebra, sheep, hawk, giraffe, dog, tiger, turtle, eel, rabbit, pig

Page 11: A-F = alligator, ball, cat, dog, egg, flashlight; G-M = guitar, hat, ice cream, jeans, ladder, mittens; N-S = nest, oar, pizza, quarter, raincoat, skateboard; T-Z = tuba, umbrella, violin, watermelon, xylophone, yak, zipper

Page 12: men, tent, ground, food, water, Abraham, child, old; laughed

Page 13: Abraham, servant, Nahor, Isaac, ten, camels, well, water, Rebekah, ring, gifts, wife

Page 14: God's love is always with me.

Page 15: I am with you and will keep you wherever you go.

Page 16: Forgiveness

Page 17: Moses means pulled from the water.

Page 18: clock, canister, flowers, television, catcher's mask, chair leg, chicken, key, upside down glass, envelope, trowel.

Page 20: For the Lord is fighting for them against Egypt.

Page 21: Mount Sinai

Page 22: Do not worship any god except me. Don't bow down and worship idols. Do not use God's name in a bad way. Remember the sabbath day; it belongs to God. Respect your father and your mother. Do not murder. Be faithful in marriage. Do not take what doesn't belong to you. Do not tell lies about others. Do not want anything that belongs to another.

Page 24: I can share with others what God has done

Page 25: afraid, locked, town wall, come in, go out, march, six, sacred chest, seventh, seven, priests, trumpets, shout, walls, fall down

Page 28: Her jars of oil and flour were never empty.

Page 30: Book of the Law

Page 33: Peace

Page 36: You will have a baby. You will name him Jesus.

Page 37: A decree went out from Emperor Augustus that all the world should be registered.

Page 38: Emmanuel, King of the Jews, Rabbi, Son of David, Good Shepherd, Son of the Most High, Savior, Lamb of God, Messiah

Page 39: In a stable

Page 40: You are my Son, the Beloved, with you I am well pleased.

Page 41: ten fish

Page 42: Caught fish

Page 43: Nothing

Page 44: canoe, row boat, raft, speed boat, sail boat, submarine

Page 46: Pick up your mat and walk.

Page 47: 12 hearts

Page 48: Jericho, Zacchaeus, tax collector, short, sycamore, down, dinner, half, four, cheated, saved

Page 49: God blesses those people who make peace.

Page 50: forgiven (blue), others (orange), judge (purple), love (yellow), good (red)

Page 51: Love your neighbor as you love yourself.

Page 52: Love one another as I have loved you.

Page 53: Forgiving

Page 54: People who listen to Jesus' teachings and obey them are wise.

Page 55: Palm Sunday

Page 56: Holy Communion

Page 58: Jesus is alive!

Page 59: 11, 2, 6, 1, 7, 8, 9, 10, 5, 12, 4, 3

Page 61: We were sent to speak for Christ.

Page 62: loving, happy, peaceful, patient, kind, good, faithful, gentle, self-controlled

Page 63: frog in a bird's nest, snake as a jump rope, square ball, heart-shaped bubble, flat flower, bear waving a flag, tree in the sky, building a snowman in summer

DIG INTO THE BIBLE